T0207678

Praise for *Create Your Space*

Said Baaghil drives brand excellence with innovative ideas and a bold spirit. A true original. Said is extremely generous in sharing his expert advice and creative vision.

> Libby Gill, Author of capture the mindshare and
> the market share will follow

It is rare to find an individual in the region with such a deep understanding of brand. Said Baaghil is truly a pioneer in this region. blazing a trail through a market riddled with agencies selling short-term marketing tactics and advertising campaigns. We applaud Said's tireless dedication to realizing the potential of Saudi Arabia's great companies. building them into the regional and global leaders they deserve to be. At Siegel+Gale, we firmly believe that in order to present a powerful and consistent brand to the world, it must sit at the center of all strategies and decision-making and act as a guide for organizational behavior. We are proud to have Said as a peer in this school of thought. and wholeheartedly support his work in enlightening individuals and executives in the Kingdom in brand marketing, aligning all marketing activities with brand strategy to build a consistent and powerful presence in the market.

> Paul Louzado, executive director,
> Siegel+Gale Middle East

An eager explorer of what's new and best in the marketing realm, Said offers his clients a thoughtful, cogent perspective on what it takes to make sure your marketing connects both rationally and emotionally with the target market. Full of energy and practical insights, Said's your guy when it comes to making it happen in marketing circles within the Middle East.

> —Dan Hill, president, Sensory Logic—US,
> author of *Emotionomics*

Said's enthusiasm and love of marketing are genuinely infectious. He brings a distinct verve to the discipline which is brought vividly to life through both his academic work and his operations. He is one of the Middle East's most vocal and powerful advocates of indigenous marketing and brand creation. both in and out of the region.

—Siobhan Adams, managing editor,
Gulf Marketing Review, Dubai

What I enjoyed most about Said's book is the helpful addition of case studies and his "no fear" attitude to bring change! Said has pivoted our brand strategy thinking by providing guidance for brands to evolve and make dynamic strategic moves so they can create their space helping them prosper. The many who read this dynamic and forward thinking book will surely benefit from user studies gone right and those gone bad. So, before you place energy into next year's marketing and brand campaign - make sure you're creating your space!

- Chris Piper, Sensory Brand Strategist

View of a brand or a market situation, and translate it in to a win for the company, the brand, and the consumer. His "Create Your Space" strategy is a smart way.

Omar Abedin, Brand Marketing pro,
author of Recovering Entrepreneur

Said, I think you have come up with a powerful and compelling approach.

David Krakoff, CEO Team Leader, Knosultwerek

Create Your Space

Transform Your Brand or Die

Said Aghil Baaghil

CREATE YOUR SPACE
TRANSFORM YOUR BRAND OR DIE

iUniverse books may be ordered through booksellers or by contacting:

iUniverse
1663 Liberty Drive
Bloomington, IN 47403
www.iuniverse.com
1-800-Authors (1-800-288-4677)

ISBN: 978-1-5320-0934-1 (sc)
ISBN: 978-1-5320-0933-4 (e)

Library of Congress Control Number: 2016917759

Print information available on the last page.

iUniverse rev. date: 10/20/2016

Contents

Acknowledgments

I believe giving credit is a way of appreciating all those who have impacted your life. So I would like to take this opportunity to thank those who have been a part of this amazing journey. I want to start with my parents. They made things possible for me in every way with the grace of God. I wouldn't be standing where I am today if it wasn't for their unconditional support and love.

To my friends who, throughout the years, made every effort to help me overcome the challenges that life threw at me, thank you for never giving up and always believing me, especially in moments when I doubted myself. To my son, you're my inspiration and hope for a better tomorrow.

This book would not have been possible without the invaluable direction of Tazeen M. Imran. She helped me to extract my most crucial thoughts by framing the strategic ideas of *Create Your Space* into words so that you, the reader, can easily understand the unconventional approach. She was not only my editor but also the project leader who put everything together. I'm so happy to have her as part of my transformational team.

I am truly grateful to Nabil Senyonga and Gwen Whitney for their valuable insights for the book and supporting my work.

I want to acknowledge Osama Natto, a Saudi passionate for

change in the way business is conducted. Osama, I admire you for the passion you hold and your vision for wanting to create impact. I hope that others are inspired by your dedication and help you create endless possibilities. Rozana Al-Banawi, I love your eccentricity and tenacity to embrace change and how you have so much love for what you do. You are a leader of change in Saudi Arabia, and I hope to see you get that chance.

Joao Moedas, my business partner of Baaghil & Diogo, we have so much to deliver from Lisbon to the world. It's so exciting to work with someone who too is a visionary and passionate about this work. I'm sure our mind-set will take us far and create the impact and change that we both have envisioned for the world.

Introduction

Who would have ever thought that companies like Kodak and Nokia would fall from the heights of glory? The strategies that made these companies iconic are, ironically, the same that led to their downfall. Advancement in technology, consumer awareness, and globalization have changed the world, and unless companies evolve, they face a fate similar to that of Kodak.

It's not enough to simply follow in the footsteps of revolutionary companies like Apple, Google, and Starbucks—but it's the best place to start. Have you ever considered why these companies are leading the market? They chose to be different and unconventional, and that is the secret of their success. Each company followed systematic strategic moves that gave them an edge over their competitors, thereby making competition irrelevant. In my fifteen years of experience as a brand and marketing strategist, I have carefully developed my own system based on their moves so that other companies can not only become successful but also lead the market. I call this strategy Create Your Space.

I thought of Create Your Space more than ten years ago, but at that time, I still needed more evidence to formulate my strategy. The true beginning of Create Your Space came in 2004, when I visited a reputable family in the Kingdom of

Saudi Arabia. I had been hired to save one of their businesses. Its high investment cost was troubling, and I had to find a way to turn it around. The initial thought I had was whether it was possible to be unconventional in a country full of conventional business habits. The only way I could convince the board members to evolve or revolutionize was to showcase the type of audience they were addressing. I carried out a focus group to gather insights into the behaviors and leisure activities of the younger generation. I was blown away by the response.

I knew from experience that there were different kinds of audiences, but they broadly fell into early adopters and late adopters. Early adopters instantly engaged with new products that others might not be familiar with. Late adopters often followed the influence of the early adopters and got acquainted with the product. With the data I had collected, I categorized participants on the basis of how likely they were to be influenced. I built everything according to the target audience and highlighted how much value the business could attain.

I presented two different ideas to the board that were in keeping with where the audience of today was going and what it desired. As the family owned a café, I first suggested redesigning the café by introducing live music, art, and better-quality food. For my second idea, I created four virtual fast-food brands. The board loved the ideas and ran with them. Five brands were created that now have an annual revenue of 36 million SAR.

In 2006, I was hired for another project—to develop an energy drink for Saudi Arabia. Initial research showed that the market was saturated with local and imported drinks and dominated by Red Bull and Bison (a local Saudi energy drink). I knew targeting to their audience would not yield any result, so I had to think of a different audience. Eventually, I did identify an audience in the lower tier. I decided to differentiate the new energy drink from Red Bull and Bison on emotional and functional values.

We kept the same price as our competitors but made some major changes. My first move was to ask R & D to benchmark Pepsi's sugar level. There were two very simple reasons for this: first, Pepsi is the preferred soft drink in Saudi Arabia because of the sweet taste, and second, the sugar level of Pepsi is higher than other energy drinks. By increasing the sugar level in our drink, I knew we would make the energy jolt stronger.

I began to notice that energy drinks were being dominated by animal names like Bison, Red Bull, and Power Horse. In order to be unique, I had to brand our product differently. I targeted the new audience by naming it Code Red. I packaged the product in a fiery red color to differentiate it from others, as the can/bottle of every other energy drink was silver and blue.

When it came to the distribution channel, I saw that my competitors were all in supermarkets and modern markets. I changed the distribution channel to sales and quick-stop shops. I knew for a fact that if wholesalers and retailers were loyal, they became the main touch points for consumers to become loyal. Instead of wasting marketing budget on advertising, I decided that a better use of the money would be to give a percentage to wholesalers and retailers on every carton sold. They also received two free cartons on orders of ten or more. The focus was on creating demand and building brand loyalty through incentives. Wholesalers and retailers had better benefits with Code Red as compared to others.

The results were phenomenal. Today, Code Red is KSA's number-one energy drink. It has an annual revenue of 600 million SAR. It is now being exported to different regions from Dubai, and it has become a case study of success for many beverage companies in KSA.

Both of these experiences taught me to think outside the box and look for ideas where others were not looking. Don't be afraid to bring changes. Look at the gaps in between. These different ideas slowly merged together and turned into a strategy. Since then, I'm known to be the most unconventional brand and marketing strategist.

The book *Create Your Space* is a result of fifteen years of work helping brands create their space. The ideas and frameworks presented here have been applied, tested, and modified over the years in the United States, Europe, and Saudi Arabia. This book not only challenges age-old methods of marketing but also shows you how to break away from them. It'll provide you with a framework to identify the core values of your brand and use them to dominate the category you are in. Throughout, I'll share case studies of both local (Saudi Arabia) and international brands that have successfully been able to create their space. At the same time, I'll include case studies of brands that didn't make it so that you can avoid doing the same.

You will notice that the book is divided into two parts. The first part will help you understand the Create Your Space concept. The second part of the book will present different case studies so that you gain perspective on what it means to create your space.

Space-creating strategy doesn't only benefit your brand, it helps the market to evolve as well. It encourages commodities to evolve into brands. One great example can set the trend for others to change. I highly recommend that every CEO and board member in the Middle East and everywhere else be aware of the values and benefits of building powerful brands. Employees and different communities look up to them as leaders. By embracing the new trends in marketing, they become catalysts for change.

Consumers in the Middle East are already looking for

this change. Foreign brands provide these consumers with diversified values, allowing them to experience the brand as an extended version of themselves. But our regional brands are too caught up in the old ways and are too comfortable with what they already know. It's only when sales decline that they feel threatened and look for a revolutionary idea to help their values evolve. By that time, it's already a bit late. We need to increase our export to places where market growth is visible, and for that, change is required.

At the heart of every leading company lie these very principles of Create Your Space. Yet most companies are unable to connect the dots because of poor understanding of these concepts. I invite you to read this book, understand how you can create your space, and embrace powerful strategic moves that will allow you to own and lead a category.

Said Aghil Baaghil

PART ONE

Own and Lead

All brand owners want their brand to become an overnight sensation. But in my experience, most of them do not even know what it takes for a brand to be successful. Some might argue that it is the logo or the name; some might claim it's the uniqueness of the product or engagement with audiences. Interestingly, we've reached a point where the old marketing gimmicks and tools are no longer impacting the audience. The dynamics of brand and marketing are changing and evolving. Advertising as we knew it has become obsolete in today's world, and consistency is not enough to make a brand relevant.

All great brands have left the used-up conventional ways and adopted innovative approaches and principles that drastically transformed their somewhat ordinary brands into unforgettable industry leaders. The first part of *Create Your Brand* shows you exactly how to break through to the other side of conventional marketing so that you can become the next industry leader in your niche area of the market.

CHAPTER 1

Old-School Marketing Is Dead

On April 1, 1976, college dropouts Steve Jobs and Steve Wozniak set up a new company that had the vision to change the way people viewed computers. They called it Apple and birthed a new era in technology. Despite having most of its features—such as hardware, software, and a digital lifestyle—in common with competitors, Apple transformed everything, including how customers used these products and perceived them as a brand. From 1976 until today, Apple has led every digital revolution that we as a global society are enjoying. This includes the billion-dollar app industry, which most mobile phone or tablet users cannot imagine life without in 2016.

Apple created its unique space in the Silicon Valley. Steve Jobs knew very well that going head-on with competitors would ensure a short shelf life for Apple as a computing and software company. So he decided to seek out a new market space, one that would make the entire ideology of competition irrelevant. As a result of Jobs' distinctive process, Apple not only evolved as a company, it revolutionized the market and influenced the way consumers use mobile phones.

The iPhone fulfilled all of our basic and intermediate

computing needs in such a way that a secondary device, such as a laptop, was made all but redundant. This regular-sized smartphone could carry out a range of tasks, handling everything from the details of an individual's day-to-day life to complex business functions. It brought great value to consumers that was very difficult to compete against. All Apple said to the world was, "Think different."

I would like to add an important underlying concept to that tagline: "Think different. Be unconventional." Apple ensures that its brand remains the most desirable in the technology market year after year through unconventional product development and marketing, I'm sure the late Steve Jobs would agree with me. Unconventionality holds great promise for the future of product branding, and I will explain how this is becoming increasingly the case.

The Rise of the New Market Space

Unlike a decade or two ago, the global arena is developing at a faster and faster rate. Brand and marketing strategies that were cutting-edge in 2015 are now struggling to keep up with even newer trends in 2016. Staying relevant is what truly matters in these exciting times. Even to a layman, it is very clear that everything from customer and user behavior to perception of different brands in different arenas to the way in which communication occurs between businesses and consumers have all been drastically transformed. Transactions and other online experiences take place instantly, via all kinds of digital platforms.

One very clear example of this new way of experiencing life is how bank transactions, online purchases, donations to charities, and other various ordering and financial services are all now completed securely with just a touch of an app. It may take some of us a while to get used to this technological explosion and how it affects every facet of human existence. This is the world's new economy, and it is very dynamic in nature.

However, it doesn't end there. The market is almost entirely jam-packed. One only has to blink and a new company comes onto the scene, claiming to be the ultimate solution-provider. I often travel to New York for business, and every time I visit there, I anticipate coming across a new coffee shop claiming to make and sell the world's best coffee. That statement has now become such a common cliché, I really don't know who to believe anymore.

In a similar fashion, with so many necessary and luxury products and their variants hitting the market, customers have most certainly moved away from what was once known as customer loyalty. A supermarket can be selling Pantene-branded shampoos, conditioners, and hair-styling products for a discounted price, and the trend now is that a lot of customers who usually prefer using Sunsilk products will pick up bottles of Pantene to store at home. Some consumers, both male and female, don't have specific hair-care needs that ensure they stick to one particular brand. They might even say, "I only want to wash my hair. This one is cheaper and has the same ingredients, so it will do the job. What difference does it make?"

These are the thinking and buying patterns that give brands nightmares. In their final attempt to increase product sales and beat the competition, the companies initiate price wars. A price war, in essence, is when every company selling hair products, for example, reduces the price to that of a competitor to tempt the consumer to choose its product based on the price. As a result of the price-lowering, profit margins are reduced, products become commodities, and everyone except the customer walks away unhappy. This is why we need to create our own space in the market so there is no longer a need to continue to indulge in these commodity wars.

The aged concept of marketing that has been around for decades hasn't really evolved. I'm sure that since the last time I checked, there will have been more detailed principles added to it to keep it tactical. It is beneficial for us to explore how marketing strategy lost the kick it once had to help companies reach their goals.

The old marketing was established during a time when industries were still developing. New products were entering categories for the first time, and they were naturally set up as leaders in their own domain. They didn't really need to focus on product categories, given there was less or no competition. Therefore they sold commodities.

Let's take the example of Kleenex. Kleenex was the first company to popularize the invention and use of facial tissue paper. Even today, facial tissue is often referred to in the United States by the name that created the category, Kleenex. If any new tissue company wished to enter the category, it would not be seen as a commodity or a product because the category had already been established. It would be known by its name or as a brand.

Another prime example is Coca-Cola. Coca-Cola established the category by introducing Coke in the late nineteenth century, when it was the first carbonated beverage sold. It was not until the early 1980s that Coke began to realize that it had some serious threats from its competitors. The consumers, instead of purchasing Coke, started to purchase diet and noncola soft drinks as health consciousness grew. This eroded Coca-Cola's market share.

After this, Coke never spoke of its product as a commodity again. Coke began associating its brand with simple and positive messages featuring universal stories with the product reflecting different aspects of the Coca-Cola experience. From its conception until today, Coca-Cola has been among the biggest brands in the world. According to Interbrand's Best Global Brand study[1] of 2015, it's the world's third most valuable brand.

Even if you're constantly evolving, it's easy to revert to the old ways when caught in the grip of your competitor's ruthless jaws. It truly becomes a jungle out there, and often companies fall into the trap of needing to compete to keep up. Staving competition off with price and other promotional tactics to achieve sales is a rule you'll find in every marketing handbook out there. When it's related to a product or a commodity, price plays a functional role. It rises and falls with market demand. When a brand constantly focuses on price, it loses its value and becomes a commodity. That's definitely not what marketing and branding are about.

What Sets Brands Apart from Commodities

Imagine you have two cars in front of you. One is a Rolls Royce, while the other is simply a car with no name. Take a minute and visualize what both of them would look like. Both are cars, and they perform the same functions. Still, a very different image comes to mind, right? That is the power of a brand.

A brand is the reference for the offerings or the business that customers come in contact with. It cultivates loyalty for and recognition of the business. In contrast, commodities are nameless, faceless products that nobody really remembers well.

When you speak of Rolls Royce or have an image of it in

---

[1] "Interbrand Releases 2015 Best Global Brand," Interbrand Newsroom, October 5, 2015, http://interbrand.com/newsroom/interbrand-releases-2015-best-global-brands-report/.

your mind, the reference is not the car as a product, because that could be any car. The reference is the name, which is the distinguishing factor. That name allows you to imagine the epitome of luxury, class, and perfection. The reason for this distinction is the values that were created by that name or the brand. Brands are all about values. It is the single thing that connects the audience with the product. Customers are forever interacting with different values of the brand. These values can be both emotional and functional.

Emotional values are inspirational values. They elicit feelings that you might experience related to the brand and your decision to purchase branded products and services. They are about what you will feel or what you will be like if you choose to engage with that brand or that product. Apple wants you to be different, Nike wants you to take action, and Starbucks wants you have the best Italian gourmet coffee experience.

Functional values refer to the product and its usability. These products exist to satisfy a functional need of the consumer. For the iPhone, functional values include the touchscreen, navigation, personal hotspot, location, App Store, and exclusive iOS. Functional values for Starbucks include flavored coffees, coffee roasts from different parts of the world, and bean grade. When creating a brand, it's vital that both emotional and functional values are at the heart of the interactive experience.

Brands That Never Made It

Not every brand will be successful. Companies repeat the same rationale over the years. The thought "What works, let it work" seems to be a settled fact with the board and management. If we look closely at the fast-moving consumer goods (FMCG) market, we'll notice similarities within each category.

Let's take the example of carbonated beverages. Pepsi and Coke are globally the two most dominant brands. Others try offering the same values and benefits, but usually this is a major disadvantage for late entries to the category because of the repetition and replication of the same values and benefits.

When new brands enter a category that has matured and offer the same values and benefits as their predecessors, they are setting themselves up for failure. Technically, customers do not see them as a unique entity, just another replication of the dominant product. There is nothing distinctive that compels the consumer to buy it.

Nokia became a sad example of this. When Microsoft partnered with Nokia for the Windows Phone, it made a critical mistake. Nokia had always been a basic phone that connected people. It was never viewed as a smartphone. Windows came quite late to the market, thinking it could compete with two powerhouses, iOS and Android, while adopting the same values and benefits. Imagine owning a phone that is completely operated by Windows, including an app store that has little compatibility with other operating systems.

A brand name is an equity registered in our mind; we associate certain images, values, and benefits with it. The name Nokia had always been viewed as a basic phone for voice and texting. The highest smartphone penetration rate[2] of 62 percent is in the age group of twenty-five- to thirty-five-year-olds. Half of all Android smartphone users and 43 percent of Apple users are below thirty-four years old, so why would a Windows phone ever appeal to the masses? For them, it's their mom and dad's phone. How uncool is that?

What should Nokia have done in this situation? All that it

---

[2]   "Smartphone Users around the World—Statistics and Facts" (infographic), Go Gulf, January 2, 2012, http://www.go-gulf.com/wp-content/themes/go-gulf/blog/smartphone.jpg.

didn't do. Nokia needed to step into the market with not only a new name but also a set of new values creating a new niche for itself if it really wanted to beat the competition.

Unfortunately, this same practice is common in the Middle East, where I come from. The market is several decades behind progressive thinking about brand and marketing. The Arabian Peninsula has witnessed trade since its earliest days—from the southern tip of Yemen to the Levant state. This trade has been carried out from generation to generation until present times. Because of that traditional mind-set of bargaining handed down through the years, business is still trapped in the trading domain, with very little grasp of what a brand is. Companies fail to understand a brand's holistic life and how it can benefit customers, consumers, and users.

The Marketing Evolution in the Middle East

Multinationals from the United States and Europe introduced brands in each category that we have in the market today: diapers (Pampers), instant coffee (Nescafé), tea bags (Lipton), tissues (Kleenex), detergent (Tide or Ariel), and toothpaste (Colgate). Each of these brands first created its space globally and is a role model for its category today. When starting out, US brands used London as their international hub to appoint distributors in the developing world, such as the Middle East and Africa. In recent years, with new developments in the educational level and changes in the infrastructure, the brands are able to create a local presence.

The precise goal of these multinationals in the region has been to lead regional sales. They are not interested in building brands because most of these brands are already established in the local category. So the sales growth requires a specific type of human capital in the companies known as *commodity marketers*. Commodity marketers' key focus is on regional sales only.

Multinationals prefer human capital with an engineering background for the purpose of following a set of rules and sticking to the core. Unlike marketing graduates, who will have opinions and ideas, engineers follow the established system very well. You'll notice that most of the heads of marketing in the region have this engineering background. They're placed in companies with the expectation that they will somehow know marketing strategies despite their years of technical experience.

With these commodity marketers in place, as we have seen in the past three decades, the region adopted a marketing concept that never evolved. The basic principle of this marketing mix heavily depended on advertising as its source of messaging and call to action. Very recently, branding became something most of the West is not familiar with: design more than strategic thinking.

The literal term *marketing* is understood as sales. The literal term *brand* is understood as a logo, and *branding* is understood as advertising. In most cases, logos are developed by designers without any strategic rationale. Rather, they are based on taste and preferences. I've actually heard cases where the logo color was changed because "My wife doesn't like blue."

Such a reality is detrimental to branding. Hardly any FMCG companies have created regional brands that sit on the shelves of a supermarket in New York City. Falafel and hummus became the origin commodity of Israel despite having roots in the Levant. Middle Eastern brands wonder why their brands are not as big as their Western counterparts.

Getting in the Space

There two different ways of becoming a brand market leader: evolution or revolution. The dictionary defines the word *evolution* as:

1. The process by which different kinds of living organism are believed to have developed from earlier forms during the history of the earth.
2. The gradual development of something.

When we talk about brand evolution, I can say it's a bit of both. Companies that plan to evolve their brand keep what is good and already working for the business, and they upgrade it to make it more relevant for a new generation, a new audience, or a new product. Before making the choice to evolve, companies must consider their brand values and explore questions like, "Will the new value connect with the same name?" Evolution focuses on improving current values and brand equity to address the new audience while staying competitive.

Let's look at McDonald's. With the increase in health awareness, McDonald's and other fast-food giants came under threat from newcomers like Five Guys and Chipotle, who were changing the fast-food market. How did McDonald's tackle this challenge? The fast-food giant undertook the biggest store-by-store makeover in the chain's history. It revamped its old image and began forming a new image in order to attract the upper-target audience of Starbucks and the like.

In making a greater effort at trust, transparency, and engagement with the audience, it launched a campaign called "Our Food, Your Questions," showing the public the quality of ingredients and the production process behind its products. Was that the right move by McDonald's for its evolution? Yes!

Without these steps, the company couldn't have retained its history and name. That would have been a huge loss.

The other way to become a market leader is through revolution. I'll go with the dictionary description again: a forcible overthrow of a government or social order in favor of a new system. Brand revolution is exactly that. It overthrows the old system and demands an entirely new business strategy. Revolution is when a company plans to enter a category and dominate it with a set of new values while broadening the range of its audience.

For an example, let's have a look at Five Guys and Chipotle. Five Guys entered the fast-food category with the intention of offering good quality food that was chemical-free and not processed. Consumers got to enjoy fresh, great-tasting fast food without the concern of added chemicals that other fast food chains like McDonald's and Burger King were using. Chipotle, meanwhile, entered the Mexican fast-food category and pushed out the idea of Tex Mex previously owned by Taco Bell by introducing a clean grilled Mexican menu. It turned to local and certified organic farms to provide healthy food for its customers.

So did these companies revolutionize their category? Yes! Did they create their market space? Yes! Are they extremely profitable? Yes! Are they massively growing? Yes! Both brands revolutionized the category by focusing on aspects that others were not paying attention to. They saw a market gap and took the opportunity to lead it. Now everyone else is either trying to catch up or follow their trend.

Evolution and revolution are not easy processes. Revolution is best for an entirely new brand, while evolution is for existing brands to address a new segment of the audience. Either way, your company must revolutionize or evolve like everything else. You need to evolve the values of your brand in order to create a niche that will bring potential growth. If not, you will just be a quick speck in history that didn't really last that long.

Brands fold faster today than ever before. Twenty years ago, who would have thought that Nokia, an industry giant, would fold or that Northwest Airlines would be taken over by Delta? No one could have imagined that McDonald's would come under threat from newbies like Five Guys.

In the coming chapter, I'll be describing what it means to create your space and how you can use that to lead your category, using key examples. As we proceed through the book, you'll start to understand that you can't hire commodity marketers, as they are not fit to evolve or revolutionize categories.

CHAPTER 2

Create Your Space

I want to claim that my strategy is totally innovative, but the truth is that Create Your Space is based on the actions of brands that succeeded in not only creating their space in the market but actually leading it—brands like Facebook, Google, Starbucks, Five Guys, Chipotle, Apple, and many others. This strategy has been tried and tested for many years by companies in FMCG, retail, hospitality, banking, and technology. It's only recently that I named the strategy and launched it in the Middle East.

The Create Your Space Model

In today's highly competitive market, a business must offer far more than just quality, price, and availability. Customers are increasingly aware, and they consider these things the basics. The Create Your Space model was developed with current market realities in mind.

To users or consumers, category will always come before brand, as it was created first. Imagine that you've decided to go to Walmart looking for some Nike shoes. You can't seem to find them, so you walk up to the salesgirl and say, "Hey,

I need some Nike shoes. Can you show them to me?" You probably wouldn't just say, "Show me Nike," because you know the salesgirl would end up asking what Nike products you are looking for.

Every category offers basic values, and most of these values are shared by all of the category participants. Many brands suffer from being too similar, giving consumers no compelling reason to buy one over the other. If a brand wants to own its category, its values must evolve so that the whole category eventually is associated with its name. Take the example of Omo, a brand of laundry detergent powder made by Unilever. In certain countries where it's known as Surf Excel, many people, rather than asking for detergent, ask directly for Surf. This is because it owns the category, so people associate detergent directly as Surf.

As I mentioned earlier, value is what really distinguishes your brand from others. Instead of focusing on what your competitors are doing or not doing, your focus should shift to creating value for consumers, thereby opening up a new space. The competition becomes irrelevant, because you are offering consumers something unique.

Create Your Space is based on these exact principles. It is a strategy that helps businesses lead and capture the category they are in. They are easily able to steer away from the cutthroat competition through a set of unique values created in the minds of their target audience. The *space* is the value that you offer. It is the reason your audience is loyal and has an affinity for your brand. In a nutshell, Create Your Space is about completely standing out and being extremely memorable without the use of advertising.

You can't own a space unless you have a unique set of values that differentiates you from your competitors. While others are fixated on benchmarking one another and maximizing their market share of the rapidly shrinking demand, Create Your Space focuses on brand dominance through evolution or revolution of the category. Brand dominance can only occur when a strong connection is created between the brand and its customers. Because of that connection, customers not only pay regular visits to the brand but also get their peers on board to buy it. According to Nielsen's "trust in advertising" report,[3] when making purchasing decisions, 84 percent of consumers are more trusting of and more influenced by their friends, family, and colleagues than any other form of advertising or engagement. The audience becomes the force that rallies behind the brand, allowing it to continue its growth.

Brands operate under the same psychology as people do. Loyalty cannot be formed by offering incentives. People will be loyal to the incentives rather than to the brand itself. Take the incentives away, and suddenly the crowd disappears. Loyalty can only be achieved when there's a connection, a trustworthy and genuine relationship between the brand and its audience. Market share will naturally follow, by default, if brand dominance is created first.

Let's return to the example of Five Guys. In 2002, when Five Guys opened its restaurant doors, it already faced competition from giant food chains like McDonald's, Burger King, and Wendy's. Menu choices were expanding beyond those of a burger joint to include higher-end salads, gourmet coffees, and chicken. Each chain tried to top the other by introducing more variety. More and more money was being invested in traditional marketing like advertising. This strategy had the

---

[3] "Under the Influence: Consumer Trust in Advertising," Nielsen, September 17, 2013, http://www.nielsen.com/us/en/insights/news/2013/under-the-influence-consumer-trust-in-advertising.html.

companies fighting amongst themselves to win customers over. The cost was going up, but there was no change in overall demand.

Given the competitive market, Five Guys had a completely different plan. It included paying absolutely no heed to what competitors were doing. The chain never hired an outside PR agency; neither did it spend a single penny on advertising. What's more, instead of following conventional marketing strategies for stepping ahead of the competition, it added a more valuable incentive by simplifying its menu and focusing on better tasting meat and fries. Amongst its list of policies at the time you would find "nothing frozen," which meant no freezers, preservatives, or chemicals. Everything was made fresh from scratch.

When McDonald's and others expanded their operations by allowing customers to order online and quickly delivering to them, Five Guys said "no delivery." It wouldn't deliver to anybody, and I mean *anybody*. In 2009, President Obama had to personally come to pick up a cheeseburger from Five Guys, a visit that made headlines and had people flocking to the chain afterward. Five Guys redefined the market by introducing completely new values, ones that were markedly different from other burger joints.

Create Your Space is about brands creating value for costumers while lowering the additional costs of marketing. Values provide people with convincing reasons why they should buy from you. This is how a leap in value for both the company and its customers is achieved.

The chart outlines the key defining features of Create Your Space in comparison to traditional marketing strategies.

Traditional Marketing Strategies	Create Your Space
Stays in current market	Creates new market space by evolution or revolution
Tries to beat competition	Sways away from competition
Functions as commodity	Focuses on values
No alignment between different aspects of the business	Aligns the whole system with the brand idea, business model, and buying audience

The Impact of Creating Your Space

William Shakespeare wrote, "What's in a name? That which we call a rose by any other name would smell as sweet." Clearly, he had no idea how powerful names—or shall I say brands—truly are. Brands matter. Leading brands like Coca-Cola are more than just products or services; they have established associations with quality and consistency. When powerful brands are establishing their unique values, they understand exactly what they are impacting. It's a systematic process where one thing leads to another. But Middle Eastern businesses are known to focus only on the bottom line.

While profit margins are part of the impact created by brands, this is not their only advantage. Companies like Apple and Google, with their innovative ideas and unique values, developed trends that changed both human behavior and lifestyle. They shaped societal opinion and offered glimpses of what the future may look like. Their impact was beyond profit margins.

When you Create Your Space with values that are right for your business, there are endless benefits. Here are some major ones you can expect to see:

- **The audience will love you.** Create Your Space is a powerful factor in driving customer loyalty, which of course determines how much market share you'll gain. While commodities are focused on winning price battles, with strong customer loyalty you can expect your audience to simply walk past those sales promotions right to you. Starbucks has one of the most loyal customer bases on the planet. The company's success and considerable new earnings have come from an app that meshes a loyalty program, My Starbucks Rewards, with payments. Upon implementing its rewards program, Starbucks saw a record-setting quarter. The program brought in more than 15 percent of US sales during the third quarter,[4] equivalent to six million weekly transactions. Analysts pointed to the increased participation in this loyalty program as the main reason. Imagine how many new people decided to walk past their old favorite coffeehouses right into Starbucks.

- **You get to dominate the brand category.** The purpose of Create Your Space is not to build a brand only but rather to create values that helps the brand dominate the category—like IKEA dominates the build-your-own

---

[4] Lauren Johnson, "Starbucks Looks to Share Its App Payment System with Other Retailers: Smartphone Transactions Supplied 15% of US Revenue in Q3," *Adweek*, July 25, 2014, http://www.adweek.com/news/technology/starbucks-looks-share-its-app-payment-system-other-retailers-159100.

furniture category, Nike dominates the sports category, and Heineken dominates the beer category.

- **You can set a premium price.** The stronger the brand, the more it is able to charge a premium price. A $10,000 Gucci bag carries the same amount of things as a $60 Aldo one. A $300 Ralph Lauren shirt probably feels as comfortable as a $35 US Polo Assn. one. But the brand equity of these companies allows them to hike up the prices for their products and earn far higher margins. If Aldo started charging $10,000 for a bag just like Gucci, chances are it wouldn't be able to sell its products the same way. This is because Aldo is not perceived in the same way as Gucci. It would have to establish certain values first that change the overall perception of the brand.

- **Brand equity brings in billions.** A brand is a valuable asset for the company that owns it. Brand equity puts you directly in the driver's seat for long-term growth. By leveraging the value offered by your brand, you can easily tap into new markets, introduce new products, and increase your profit streams. Household names like Gap and Forever 21 make the highly exclusive rich list. In 2014, they had a combined wealth of $34.75 billion.[5] All successful brands that created their space share these benefits. Create Your Space is an investment that will continue to pay back on its own in numerous ways as your company evolves and grows.

---

[5]   Chloe Sorvino, "America's Richest Fashion Billionaires—and the Brands That Just Miss the Mark," *Forbes*, October 1, 2014, http://www. forbes.com/sites/chloesorvino/2014/10/01/americas-richest-fashion-billionaires-and-the-brands-that-just-miss-the-mark/#75fbfad44014.

Building Momentum to Create Your Space

There's no confusion about the significance of creating your own space. There is a general understanding that the chances for success are far higher when you create your space than when companies venture into categories by replicating values of the dominant brand. Of course, this doesn't mean that by implementing Create Your Space, you will be risk-proof and your brand will be set for life. Implementing strategies always involves certain risks. General guidelines always need to be in place for risk mitigation in order to enhance opportunities and reduce threats.

The success rate of brands depends on a number of factors. One of the key factors is the company's willingness to evolve. If there is little or no willingness to change, then strategy itself cannot help the brand. I design the strategy in a way that the flow of it, from top to bottom, has its own sets of rules. Sometimes that means letting go of a lot of old ways that companies are used to. Those who are willing to change to keep up with the changing world wholeheartedly embrace them, while others are not willing to adopt the new ways of working. How strategy is carried out is the responsibility of the company.

Another major reason strategies fail is because they are handed over to a person who designs a super-flashy expensive new website and logo for the company or to a business executive who recently came back from London feeling inspired. Bottom line, the right candidate for the job isn't the one driving the strategic change.

Just recently, I was hired as an advisor to go through a marketing strategy by a former employee of a leading multinational. I spent all afternoon trying to figure out where the strategy, purpose, and specialization were. I was only able to see the types of communication and audiences they were addressing. There was absolutely no strategy in place. When I get cases like these, I can't help but wonder if there's confusion between marketing strategy and marketing plan, or if somehow strategy has been redefined in the Middle East and I missed out on that memo.

You can't really expect a fish to dance outside of its fish bowl. Implementing a strategy requires someone who is very familiar with how it works, because it's not a one-size-fits-all model. Each organization's strategy is different. While this book will be introducing the framework briefly, I would advise you to proceed with caution and find the right candidate to implement this. That is very important.

Now let's move on to Chapter 3, which introduces the main framework required to create your space.

The Framework for Create Your Space

I have spent the past decade trying to develop a framework in an attempt to make the formulation and execution of Create Your Space as systematic and methodical as possible, so that any brands that wish to use this framework can easily evolve or revolutionize their category. I then applied and tested this in action by working with companies who wanted to create their space, enriching and refining the framework in the process.

In this chapter, we will be talking about how we can implement the framework by identifying key factors of Create Your Space. I will explain the role and importance of each implementation factor. Companies can evolve or revolutionize the industry or market fundamentals through the purposeful application of these factors.

Create Your Space is based on a five-step framework. Let's look at each of those steps in some detail.

Step 1: Getting Started

The first step to creating your space is to identify the activities, decisions, and relationships critical to accomplishing that. For this, you'll conduct a spatial audit, which provides an internal and external insight. The spatial audit is a diagnostic tool and an action framework for Create Your Space, and it captures the current state of your organization. This allows you to understand your own human resources, financial resources, organizational structure, and readiness to evolve.

Step 2: Finding the External Market

Once the internal spatial audit is done, the second part of the framework focuses on identifying the external market in order to break from the competition. Usually this is the part that companies struggle with. The challenge is to successfully identify, out of the endless possibilities that exist, opportunities to evolve or revolutionize the category. This step is crucial if companies don't want their strategies to be based on guesswork or luck.

The intention is to have relevant data that will help solve marketing problems your brand might encounter. In order to find the external market, you need to scope out the size of your industry, learn about your competitors, asses the nature and maturity of the category, and figure out opportunities based on your target audience.

Step 3: Creating Big Ideas

After the external market, the opportunity, and your internal ability to deliver have been identified, you can move on the next step of the framework: creating a big idea for your brand. When Steve Jobs launched the iPod, he called it "a thousand songs in your pocket." He didn't have to explain any further. Everyone was ready to buy it. Imagine if he'd said, "This is an mp3 player that will help you listen to your songs." We would have been bored in a second.

Apple has never focused on pitching products; instead, it sells innovation. Everything Apple does is based on innovation, and it sells that idea every day. We no longer speak of commodities or products—these days, we speak of the idea associated with the brand. The brand becomes synonymous with the perception and the idea that is created in the minds of consumers. This idea is built throughout the customer journey, starting from the initial contact through the process of engagement and into a long-term relationship.

Think of Nike. It is not just selling sport shoes. There are probably companies that make better shoes than they do. But when people buy Nike shoes, they aren't simply buying shoes, they're buying the idea of empowering performance. Nike has become synonymous with athletics, fitness, and health. That's why you see sport celebrities like Michael Jordan associated with the brand. When you wear those shoes, you feel inspired and motivated. In the same way, Disney doesn't sell rides, characters, or the movies, it sells magic.

You need to think about the uniqueness of the idea within the category, as well as the distinctive values and experiences the idea has to offer. It must be a revolutionary idea that brings new values as a trend to the category while resonating with the audience. When we think of the idea, we must ask the following questions:

- Is the idea scalable and able to evolve over a number of years to increase revenue?
- Does the idea resonate perfectly with the current audience?
- Can the idea evolve with new values to address a future audience?

- Is the idea both inspiring and realistic in its nature?
- Does the idea address both need and want?
- Does the idea have unique values that create market space?

If you focus solely on the product, then you're not selling a brand, you're selling a commodity. Products are only a part of what you sell; what you really need to focus on is selling the idea of what the brand is all about.

Step 4: Finding the Right Audience

In today's world, it's impossible to address all of the audience in general. People have different backgrounds, interests, habits, and behaviors. Some customers might want the best price while others might look for high-end products. It's impossible to cater to them all. This is why, in the fourth step of Create Your Space, you need to divide a large audience into smaller groups of people—or segments—that have similar needs, values, or characteristics.

By identifying your segment, you can find loyal followers who will resonate with your brand. For example, Apple speaks to the cool, creative designers who are truly loyal to the brand. Five Guys speaks to the fresh, food-conscious audience. FedEx speaks to corporates who need fast courier service overnight.

Focus is the key in Create Your Space. Everything must be focused, from the big idea to revenue to the audience. Things to consider while identifying the audience are:

- Identify a segment of the audience that will resonate with your idea and revenue stream.
- Focus on those who will respond quickly and those who will join later on.

- Frequently monitor their feelings about the big idea.
- Keep improving values based on the audience's reaction.

Most marketers focus on demographics, such as age and income. In Create Your Space, the audience forms an emotional rapport with the idea. Customers become advocates for the brand and start to promote the product or service by word of mouth, which leads to increased opportunities to create loyal followers.

We don't determine who the customer is before the launch. The initial market reaction, after the launch, will determine the type of audience we have. It's really after six months that we find our true segment. We then focus on who's loyal and how big the segment is. We grow according to the growth of the segment.

Step 5: Identifying the Revenue Stream

Now that we have discussed the other components of Create Your Space, it's time to look at revenue stream, the final step to the framework. It is the building block representing how much money you can generate. Businesses can be broken into two categories: low-margin and high-margin. The primary difference is in the core of the business model itself, and this is readily apparent to any brand strategist. Many times companies aim for the mass and commodity markets instead of evaluating their place.

In low-margin businesses, products sell for close to the price it costs a company to build and maintain the product. Gross profit margins are low. This generally leads to a high product turnover. To stay efficient, the price must be competitive, and the company must be able to sell a high volume of goods.

With high-margin businesses, products may be sold at a much higher price than the actual cost of the product.

However, products sold are fewer in this model compared to lower-margin businesses. Most businesses prefer this approach, however, to avoid the complexity of the logistics.

Questions to consider regarding revenue stream include the following:

- Does your idea resonate with high-margin or low-margin? If the history of the existing business is low-margin, you must stick to the same revenue stream. The nature of the profit margin can't be changed, otherwise the entire organization will have to change
- Does the idea and audience dictate the profit margin model, or is it the other way round?
- Irrespective of which margin it is, does the margin resonate with the values and the proposed idea of the business? If not, they will carry different purposes

Let's take a look at some examples of revenue streams. Gold's Gym International, Inc., is an American chain of international co-ed fitness centers originally started in California by Joe Gold. Gold's Gym offers three revenue streams for membership: bronze, silver, and gold. Each membership type is based on a specific segment need and income.

Then we have IKEA, the world's largest furniture retailer. The big idea behind IKEA is assembling your own furniture. The revenue-stream statement is marketing premium-stylish furniture at a low price. This is a low-margin revenue where products are sold at a competitive price. IKEA is able to generate a huge volume of goods at a low price while maintaining high profit margins.

So there you have it: the framework for Create Your Space. It's simple enough but often difficult to achieve. It takes a lot of commitment and determination to witness organic growth without the use of advertising. The purpose of an unconventional idea in communication is to generate instant buzz with the media and public. Once the steps are identified, you can move to the brand and marketing strategy that will support the Create Your Space model.

In the next chapter, I'll highlight some of the barriers that companies have set up for themselves. When an organization is aiming to evolve or revolutionize its category, regardless of industry, it must be more than willing to take on these barriers in order to succeed. Only then can it fulfill the brand's true potential.

CHAPTER 4

Overcoming the Barriers

As I've met different people in different organizations over the past fifteen years, I've grown used hearing, "Whatever you said was great, Said, but if you were in my company, you'd know how tough the situation truly is." When I initially started out, I was always confused by this. Sometimes in my head I would think they were just being change-resistant, and I even considered them a bit boneheaded. I couldn't understand why it was so hard to bring in these changes. I thought to myself, "Why wouldn't any company want to own or lead its category?" It just didn't make sense.

Over time, however, I saw a pattern. It wasn't that they were being stubborn but rather that they were stuck in traditional ways of doing things and couldn't understand how to get out of it. My strategies made sense, but these individuals lacked the clarity and capability to implement change one way or another. That's why they would agree with me but at the same time share why it would be hard to follow through.

In this chapter, I'll be sharing with you the most frequent "Yes, but …" things I have seen or heard. These are the barriers that stop organizations from implementing Create Your Space. For each barrier, I'll describe the red zone—the risks, dangers, and consequences an organization faces—and propose a solution that can help you break through.

Sales Targets

Many companies across the Middle East believe themselves to be brands with unique values. But despite being a brand, they can't seem to achieve their sales target. They claim that being a brand doesn't really make any difference.

The Red Zone

These companies complain that they are big brands and have made huge efforts to develop their sales plans, including choosing the right techniques, breaking down large goals into smaller targets, and setting activity goals. They have followed every rule in the marketing book, and still, sales targets are not being achieved. So it comes as no surprise that they think being a brand makes no difference.

Companies need to understand that the sales process goes way beyond sales plans and targets. The marketing mix must be well aligned with the brand's values so that it offers a unique set of experiences. Skilled talent must be in place to drive innovation and customer service, create growth opportunities, and mitigate risks.

More often than not, I see that the company has not invested in hiring qualified people. Sales departments are filled with greenhorns who have no idea how to even make a pitch. To make matters worse, there is inadequate coaching and skill development. Because employees don't fully understand how products benefit the customers and how to build rapport with their audience, it's likely performance will be poor.

As for the sales plan, the vision is usually focused on

short-term growth. I know companies have financial restraints, but I have seen them splurging on advertising so they can ride the benefits of that one great product they've put out in the market. When the hype is over, they really don't know how to sustain growth in the long term.

Focusing on short-term sales is like running a marathon with your head down, looking only the few meters ahead of you. As you focus all your concentration on where you are stepping, you lose sight of the ultimate target and fail to see what lies ahead of you on the road. With little or no anticipation for the future, companies end up being unprepared for what comes their way. It's no surprise when they struggle to win against their competitors.

Management and the board usually put a great deal of pressure on marketing and operations to push sales. In most cases, this results in brands turning into commodities. They attain huge sales but often at a low margin.

The Solution

Sales targets not being achieved is not the root cause of trouble but rather a symptom. The first step to overcoming the problem is becoming aware of what is really happening underneath the surface. A lot of companies are in denial. They prefer to look at themselves as brands when in reality they are commodities.

Even though companies think they have unique values, they usually fail the litmus test when I put them through it. As we discussed earlier in the book, there is a certain framework that needs to be in place for a company to be a brand. It's not what you say it is, it's what the perception is in the eyes of the customer. Let's admit it, we only remember two kinds of brands: the ones we love and the ones we hate. There is no middle ground. They simply fade into each other.

If you really want to understand whether your company is a brand or not, I suggest you create a checklist and go through the framework I have offered in Chapter 3. See if you have those elements in place. If you do, then calculate the extent to which they exist. This will provide you with a brief idea of where you stand as a brand.

Brands are the result of everyday sales and customer loyalty. Focusing on your brand will help your sales remain constant and give you the opportunity to grow. Once you have this opportunity, raise the standard of your human capital by investing in and developing them. Companies need to maintain their brand focus, deliver the values of the perceived price, and make sure to take their staff along for the ride.

Personal Agendas

There's an age-old problem in the Middle East: the companies are dominated by the owner's or CEO's personal preferences, with a bit of local tradition and few business strategies thrown in. CEOs and management end up following their own agendas instead of focusing on business strategies. The company is divided up into smaller interest groups that follow their leader's agenda rather than sticking to what's best for the business. This makes it difficult for a company to be fluid and a brand to reach its full potential.

The Red Zone

Consider the following analogy: A company works like a ship. Before the ships starts to sail, the captain has already planned where it is going, how he will get the ship there, and what needs to be done. The crew is informed and aligned with those decisions before the ship sets out to sea. Now imagine a captain who keeps changing the plan over and over again. With no sense of psychological security, some of the crew would end up feeling demotivated and frustrated with the captain and the ship. Others would try to salvage whatever opportunities they can get out of the situation and form their own groups. This might result in inner conflicts and ultimately a mutiny.

The same goes for companies. Indecision and politics are very costly to the company, affecting it both internally and externally. Internally, employees become frustrated, which invites turnover, absenteeism, grievances, bad press, and costly internal and external lawsuits. Because the internal departments are torn by conflict, the company has less time to focus on building the brand. This, in turn, affects the brand itself, because it's unable to grow from within the company.

Furthermore, if choices are based on preferences and then changed accordingly, a brand cannot be sustained even in the short term. The Pareto principle states that roughly 20 percent of causes generally account for 80 percent of results. This means that roughly 20 percent of the decisions you make will account for 80 percent of the impact that you sooner or later face. This theory holds true for brands as well.

Imagine the management has come up with some unique values for the brand which would fall in the category of the 20 percent. Because there is internal conflict, there's argument over what those values might be. This would make the entire decision process come to a halt, resulting in the 80 percent impact. Decisions are always made in alignment with what the brand stands for. In this case, because the values are not clear, important decisions related to the brand would be made on guesswork. This obviously jeopardizes growth and even threatens to make the brand to decline and eventually shut down.

The Solution

Breaking a culture of preferences requires a leader who can engender intellectual honesty, connect with the higher purpose, and strategically plan ahead for the years to come. But leadership itself needs to promote a culture of change. Gwen Whitney-Gill, manager of coach development at College for America, had this to share with us on how companies can develop a culture of change:

> Establishing a positive "Culture of Change" requires a deliberate and flexible mindset. Change, while important to development and growth, can be uncomfortable or even fear provoking. In this "Culture of Change," there are both leaders and the employees. Each role is integral to success.
>
> Effective leaders learn to accept, understand and embrace "Resistance" as an important part of the process. It is important to highlight that "Resistance" is different than "Reluctance." Reluctance is an unwillingness to engage in the conversation of change. Resistance comes about as a result of wanting to understand, but needing more information prior to engagement. Managing resistance requires effective and consistent communication and an open mindset around questioning and being questioned.
>
> One does not need to be in a leadership role to positively influence this culture. As a participant in the culture of change, one must be ready to reflect and consider what impact

you can have. Often thoughts or questions related to resistance sound much like the following:

"Can I contribute as equally to something new as I have to our established practice?"

"How does change impact my identity within the organization?"

"Does the goal of this change line up with the values of my organization or the values of my work?"

One must consider what questions might arise around reluctance when developing a communication plan. Engaging in this exercise will assist in ensuring clarity around how new goal(s) align with the values of an organization. Commitment to a positive culture of change requires regular connection between the stated vision and values. Regardless of the role one plays, continue to check in with yourself and others. Examine resistance, identify reluctance, and establish values connection.

It's important to recognize that the culture needs to be changed in order for the brand to grow.

No Understanding of Brands

Most CEOs and management still do not fully understand what brands are. They are under the impression that registering a logo as a trademark and then using advertising to sell the product or service is all it takes to be a brand. They lack a clear understanding of brand dynamics.

The Red Zone

In today's world, brands are built on the interaction between the company and the customers. If the CEO is only focused on the design of the website and shape of the logo, the brand will not be able to identify the values through which it can grow. If the value proposition isn't clear, a logo and a website isn't going to help. If people don't understand the values the brand is offering, they are unlikely to buy it.

Loyal customers consistently do business with their preferred brands, often ignoring convenience or pricing factors. These loyal customers are also more likely to tell friends and family about the brand, creating a stream of new customers. By opting to exclusively focus on driving the next purchase, CEOs lose the opportunity to dominate the category they are in.

The Solution

Leaders of organizations that have built high brand equity over time emphasize the brand's values. They understand that they are the focal point of demonstrating these values and must lead by example and demonstrate consistent behavior. They need to own their brand's beliefs and communicate them across the company. Through this role-modeling, employees emulate similar behaviors. Living the brand values helps employees live up to the brand promise, knowing what they need to deliver to make the brand a magnet for customers.

CEOs, like everyone else in the organization, are brand ambassadors. From assistant managers through the CEO, brand awareness and knowledge is now essential. These executives must be coached to thrive in a time where customer interaction is so close to the brand. CEOs attract the most publicity with their words and behaviors. With the right kind of attitude, they can lead their brand toward a new vision.

Lack of Innovation

I have seen that most organizations in the Middle East lack the innovation culture and live on what market dictates them.

The Red Zone

There are a lot of lost opportunities for companies that do not innovate. If a company has failed to bring in new ideas that are vastly different, creative, advanced, or unique, customers will have no points of distinction when they compare the company with its competitors. It will be just another face in the crowd. Over time, this will erode the company's market position because it will not be at the forefront of the next big wave in the industry. Sticking with the status quo instead of innovating will result in a loss of revenue.

Brands that were once household names have vanished simply because they failed to evolve with the world around them. They decided to stay the same, refusing to act. If companies fail to innovate, they offer the basic value of the category and drive the brand to become a commodity and ultimately attain low margins.

The Solution

All innovative activities depend on the behavior of employees. Great minds are critical to innovation and essential for a brand's future. Google is a prime example of this. Laszlo Bock, senior vice president of Google's people operations, mentioned in "Google's Secrets of Innovation: Empowering Its Employees"[6]—an article in *Forbes* magazine—that there

---

[6] Laura He, "Google's Secrets Of Innovation: Empowering Its Employees," March 29, 2013, http://www.forbes.com/sites/laurahe/2013/03/29/googles-secrets-of-innovation-empowering-its-employees/#67fbc3b7eb39.

were different channels through which employees could express creativity. They included:

- Google cafés, which are designed to encourage interactions between employees within and across teams and to spark conversation about work as well as play
- direct emails to any of the company's leaders
- intensive coaching and support
- soliciting feedback on hundreds of issues and getting the entire company to solve them

Nabil Senyonga, who as founder of Senyonga and Associates advises clients on organizational culture, shares this on how to develop great minds for the organization:

> To win in any team sport, professionals know that they need a game plan. That game plan needs to be unique and proprietary to you so it differentiates you from the rest and the more eccentric and unconventional you are, the more you stand out from the crowd. The same applies to organizations and individuals. However, being successful means that that after setting your strategy/game plan you know how to deploy your talents and resources to maximum potential, as it would be very difficult to "win" if you don't have that path.

Business leaders will go all out on developing the game plan but undermine the talent management. What's needed is a deep-rooted belief among business leaders that people really matter—that leaders must develop the capabilities of employees, nurture their careers, and manage the performance of individuals and teams.

You can define a great organization by its brand recognition; however, at the heart of that organization is a culture that has been developed based on harnessing the success of its people. That's what makes the organization great. Companies can create this culture of talent development alongside their strategy deployment by:

- acting as a role model
- reinforcing the value of learning
- building sustainable processes to support development
- reinforcing shared values
- leveraging problems as opportunities for real-world learning and development

When developing the company's strategy, we need to look beyond the obvious points like profitability, market share, approval ratings, and customer satisfaction, and focus on making talent a strategic priority. In order to evolve or revolutionize, companies need to diversify their human capital to serve the overall vision of the brand. The more diverse and progressive employees are, the more ideas and thoughts will percolate up, giving the company a truly creative outlook.

Most organizations focus on the barriers instead of the solution. As human nature dictates, they are in denial of the red zone and the long-term consequences. However, I admit, oftentimes the solution is not easy and requires a complete transformation of the company, which means the CEO and management could be at risk too. Failing to understand how brands work and handing the complete responsibility to the head of marketing often is a recipe for failure. I say very confidently that 99 percent of marketers—including multinationals in the Middle East—have a very basic understanding of brands. But that doesn't mean we ignore what is present and sacrifice our future for short-term gratification. It just doesn't work that way. You must transform your organization—otherwise, with such rapid changes, it will gradually die.

PART TWO

Brand Studies

To understand how Create Your Space works, I will be discussing different brands from different industries. It is important to understand how each of these brands evolved, revolved, or devolved in its category. These examples will give you the opportunity see what your company needs to do more of—and what to avoid.

My analysis is my personal point of view of how the strategy could have been different. I in no way claim to have directly worked with these companies or influenced them. I would just like to use them as examples so that you can understand Create Your Space even better.

CHAPTER 5

Apple—The Game Changer?

Back in the late nineties, Nokia's communicator and Microsoft's i-mate were the hottest products in the cell phone industry. The communicator was a huge handheld device that looked like a normal phone on the outside and opened in a clamshell format to access a QWERTY keyboard and an LCD screen inside. It was a business-optimized phone that organized data and sent emails. While fulfilling the same functions, i-mate was more contemporary and targeted the younger generation. The category hadn't really evolved at that time and was still known by the functional name *mobile*. However, both products made an impact on the category because, for the first time, business-optimized phones were being used by executives rather than the usual phones.

After a few years, the Canadian brand BlackBerry hit the market, catering to a wider audience that included both youth and corporate executives. It introduced new values with the BlackBerry Messenger, through which you were able to connect with your work and friends whenever you needed to. This was a game-changer. The mobile category evolved from a talking device to something more social through texting, and the smartphone was born.

This new value took BlackBerry to the top. But it wasn't enough to hold it there. At this stage, social media stepped in, and most people were using social platforms like Facebook, LinkedIn, and Twitter. Yet using social media on the mobile phone was unheard of at the time. As the smartphone category matured, Apple came up with the idea for an innovative phone. In 2007, Steve Jobs, CEO of Apple, said, "Today, Apple is going to reinvent the phone." Jobs said that he was going to introduce a "widescreen iPod with touch controls," a "revolutionary mobile phone," and a "breakthrough Internet communicator."

He wasn't talking about three different products here but a single product that combined three devices. The iPhone was far more than just a cell phone. An entirely new value came into play and changed the nature of the category. Apple catered to the demand of the new generation. It had an exclusive iOS and an app store on the phone. This reinforced the impression that Apple was innovative, and so was Steve Jobs. But this was not enough to keep even the iPhone on top.

Soon Google launched an open-source operating system, Android. Because this wasn't what iPhone and iOS were offering, Google was able to break into the market and create its space. Samsung, which wanted its own high-end smartphones to compete with the iPhone, decided to run Android. Samsung began beating its competitors one at a time, starting with HTC, then Motorola, then BlackBerry, and finally Apple. Its campaign "the next big thing" propelled the idea—for the first time since the launch of the iPhone—that there was something better out there that Apple wasn't offering. People loved it, helping Samsung become one of the best-selling smartphone brands in the world.

Samsung dominated the functional aspect of the smartphone category, which rested on product value and price. Meanwhile, iPhone continued to dominate the emotional side of the category, which was based on the entire experience of brand along with the functional aspect of the product values.

Think "Create Your Space"

So how did Apple create its space? The company revolutionized the idea of the phone, changing it from a tool for talking into a social platform for all types of communication. Apple introduced many unique values, like the App Store, iPod music, and a rotating camera. The company continued to focus on innovation, winning the hearts and loyalty of millions.

That continued until Steve Jobs' death. Fast forward to 2015, and Tim Cook showed something that the audience was already expecting. The style and hype of the delivery tried to cover a growing problem: Apple has run out of creative juices. Apple's core essence as a brand is no longer the same.

Today, Apple faces the same threats that others face because, in the past three years, it failed to renew or recreate the values that put it ahead of the competition. If Apple continues on the same path, then sooner or later it might end up like Microsoft, which lost its innovative edge after Bill Gates left.

If you remember, we discussed Microsoft's strategic mistakes in Chapter 1 under "Brands That Never Made It." I feel Apple is not too far from repeating history.

CHAPTER 6

The Changing Face of Uber

Recently, Uber switched to a new logo, and fans around the world were not pleased. Instead of the stylized white and black "U" that it once was, the new design integrated what the company calls the "atom and bit." It caused quite a stir on social media platforms like Twitter and Instagram, with many quick to declare the app icon ugly. So can Uber change its image and still stay strong?

Think "Create Your Space"

I say yes! As we discussed earlier in Chapter 1, in order to create its space, a brand either needs to evolve or revolutionize a category. Uber is a perfect example of how a brand first revolutionized the category and then continued its evolution. It identified a gap in the market and jumped in to fill it. Uber created a whole new system by relying on technology to connect users with service providers.

Uber created its space by tackling the whole experience of the cab infrastructure and service—including unmaintained cabs, unreliable customer service, late cars, no flexible payment options, and more. It sought to offer a luxury car service that was convenient and didn't cost $800 for a ride—a price that

Travis Kalanick, CEO of Uber, once paid. It changed what was once an experience offered only by limousine services into an on-demand cab alternative easily accessible through a smartphone app. Through this app, Uber redesigned the entire cab experience, allowing customers different payment options, better cars, freedom from tipping, and the ability to rate drivers and help other riders decide who to go with.

Criticizing Uber's new logo is pointless. Brands are not just based on design. They are much larger than that. The brand idea and values of Uber are its brand equity, not the image that changed from a "U" to an "atom and bit."

Design is a representation of the perception of the brand. It is an image to lure the audience to experience the brand. It eventually becomes a reality based on the idea, the value, and the experience it offers. In Create Your Space, the image of what the brand stands for is important, but it is not important enough to change the life of the brand. Logos do matter, but not more than the values that the company stands for. I remember when Google's new logo came out in 2015, people made a major fuss over it, predicting that Google was killing its brand. Almost a year later, Google is as strong as ever.

Uber lost equity because of its recent identity revolution. However, this was needed because its business model and values have completely changed. The company evolved with a new value proposition, even updating its tagline from "Everyone's private driver" to "Where lifestyle meets logistics" in order to fulfill current and future needs. It's not a cab service anymore. It's the future of logistics, and its new identity is a reflection of this.

CHAPTER 7

The Curious Case of Rabea and the Millennials

Rabea is a heritage brand known for many years in Saudi Arabia as the king of loose-leaf tea. Recently, the company decided to evolve its product propositions, including most of the SKUs like the long-leaf, to fit the category and chase the millennial audience. Was this the right move?

Think "Create Your Space"

No. It's sad to see a prestigious brand with a lineage of more than sixty years trying to fill up the shelves with line extensions rather than creating its space. The evolution needs to start with the brand, not the propositions. Rabea, instead of focusing on its brand, moved in with line extensions. It's the brand that dictates the audience, not the product—unless Rabea planned on being a commodity.

The values offered by the brand are transformed into customer experience. The once-prestigious brand that was used in every Saudi household has now become a commodity overshadowed by line extensions, availability, and price. After replicating Lipton's strongest brand signal, the tea bag, Rabea became the second choice for consumers. Today, the majority of Rabea's SKUs are in tea bags. Instead of Rabea creating its space, it decided to compete with the category's strongest brand.

How could Rabea have created its space? When you have a new audience to address, such as millennials, in order to propose a unique set of values, you would need to revolutionize the category first. The name, tone, and relevance of Rabea resonates well with traditional values, families, and the older generation. Millennials want a glimpse of a better life, inspiration, and happiness. That is anything but traditional.

Millennials are everywhere on social media—Facebook, Twitter, Instagram. While there are many platforms on which a brand can catch their attention, it's the brands that differentiate themselves that end up winning customers in the right way, by creating a deep connection. For this, both brand and marketing strategy have to be relevant to the audience.

Rabea, instead of being the fatherly figure with a legacy, should have created a sub-brand with values relevant to today's audience. The pillars of the entire brand—such as knowledge, differentiation, self-esteem, and relevance—are nowhere in Rabea's new evolution. In fact, Rabea lost the brand's self-esteem with a new set of values that were already owned by Lipton and others. Rabea is a great brand overall, but not a brand that evolved to suit the millennial audience. Things it could do to rectify that include the following:

- Instead of following trends and filling up shelves, innovate some of the existing values to build relevance to a new audience.
- Tea, unlike coffee, is seen as boring. Develop excitement for the experience and offer values that lead to a new culture.

- Revisit the current brand strategy and evolve it to address the current audience.
- The name Rabea resonates with the past. The new audience wants a name that resonates with its way of life

We are in an era of big brands, not commodities. Fitting SKUs into a clutter category is a trade-marketing mind-set, not brand evolution.

CHAPTER 8

Turning Al Nahdi into a Brand

Al Nahdi is a local Saudi medical company that has grown dramatically to become the largest retail pharmacy chain in the Middle East and North Africa. It has always been known as a pharmacy. In recent years, it decided to reposition itself as a health and wellness company. In order to revolutionize and create its space, it underwent an aggressive change in logo, website, and emphasis.

Think "Create Your Space"

Usually audiences highly resonate with idea a company tries to sell. But in the case of Al Nahdi, that is not happening. The company wants to be known for health and wellness, while consumers still treat Al Nahdi as a pharmacy. Such a goal requires an entire category change, which could also mean losing equity with the pharmacy category. Since the transformation requires changing categories, the heart of the brand strategy will need to be transformed as well, and that includes dropping the name Al Nahdi, since it resonates as a pharmacy.

I'm not aware of the internal affairs involved, but there are two different scenarios that could have occurred based on my understanding. First, the head of marketing and management must have had a very basic understanding of brand strategy. The failure to grasp the difference between branding and advertising is often what creates a marketing gap. In the Middle East, there is a misperception that launching a new identity on billboards and other places means that the audience will start treating the company differently and that the company has successfully switched between the categories.

The second scenario I can imagine is that, like many other Middle Eastern companies, the name belongs to the family. The owners and the board probably decided to change nothing, thereby forcing marketing to drive the brand based on old Al Nahdi pharmacy attributes. I will say, in this case, that the marketing department seems clearly inexperienced when it comes to revolutionizing the brand strategy, while both the board and the management seem to be clueless regarding the brand values.

So while Al Nahdi splurged on advertising, it was unable to get its audience to connect to its new values. The goal was to evolve from a pharmacy to a company that stood for health and wellness. There was nothing unique for the audience to connect to with the new identity. The company might have designed its logos to highlight the new feel, but for me it seems that they didn't design a brand strategy, so the transition into the new category remains in oblivion.

CHAPTER 9

The Evolution of Al Baik

Al Baik is a well-known fast-food chain in Saudi Arabia that primarily sells deep-fried broasted chicken. The founders are very people-oriented and work with humility, integrity, and conscientiousness. As a brand throughout the years, Al Baik has appeared and been experienced as humble, caring, and charitable. It has touched many people's lives through its community work and activities.

Recently, Al Baik decided to evolve from the fresh home look and feel—something that has greatly resonated with the locals and people of all incomes—to what McDonald, KFC, Pizza Hut, Burger King, and others have looked and felt like for years. So what went wrong here?

Think "Create Your Space"

Instead of building on the old brand attributes, Al Baik decided to bring in the values of other fast-food joints. At a time when brands like McDonald's were evolving to address today's concerns over junk food and becoming more health conscious, Al Baik unfortunately decided to move in the opposite direction. The new locations of Al Baik look and feel the same as McDonald's did to most.

Al Baik never really sold chicken. If the battle was only focused on chicken, KFC and others options were available too. Al Baik as a brand represented great-quality, fresh, homemade chicken with a secret recipe that the audience across the Kingdom of Saudi Arabia loved. The brand attributes for decades had been humility, caring, and altruism.

When Al Baik decided to evolve and expand its channels, it should've carried along the brand attributes that made it what it is. Quality of food alone was never the whole story; it was about the entire experience. Al Baik once owned a space, and now it has opened the space and provided an opportunity for others to enter.

Epilogue

After reading these real business examples, I hope that you've become aware of the importance of creating your space. Brands that embark on a journey of revolution and continue their evolution sustain growth and experience true success. They do not allow themselves to turn into commodities. In other cases, it's clear to see that companies are heading in a direction where they will be fighting with competitors to gain space in the market. All these cases clearly show that it's up to the CEO and the management of the company to champion the transformation journey of the brand and create the greatest impact in the category.

I have seen many businesses stagnate and fold because they failed to listen to the advice of market experts and remained in denial about the changing business world around them. I understand that change is hard, but in today's uber-competitive world, if you are not evolving and changing, you are setting yourself up for failure. I hope after reading *Create Your Space*, you will be inspired to break the mold of traditional marketing and use this strategy to evolve your current business and move forward.

This book has presented an unconventional approach to creating your own market space. I'm optimistic that the steps I have illustrated have shown you how essential it is to know the values your brand stands for. The shared examples and advice from different industries provide valuable insights for your exciting journey ahead. I'm confident that when you start implementing Create Your Space, you'll set your business on a path of revolution that separates you from your competitors while helping you evolve.

From this point onward, you need to decide where your company is heading and which category would suit you best in order to maximize opportunities. I assure you, in this competitive market, nothing will sustain your business unless you're unconventional. So I would like to leave you with Apple's 1997 "Think Different" ad campaign, which celebrated the rule-breakers and troublemakers who push humanity forward:

> *Here's to the crazy ones.*
> *The misfits.*
> *The rebels.*
> *The troublemakers.*
> *The round pegs in the square holes.*
> *The ones who see things differently.*
> *They're not fond of rules.*
> *And they have no respect for the status quo.*
> *You can quote them, disagree with them, glorify or vilify them.*
> *About the only thing you can't do is ignore them.*
> *Because they change things.*
> *They push the human race forward.*
> *While some may see them as the crazy ones, we see genius.*
> *Because the people who are crazy enough to think*
> *they can change the world, are the ones who do.*
> © 1997 Apple Computer, Inc.

I hope you, too, adopt the unconventional mind-set and in your own way leave an impact on your category for the world to see.